Barnyard Pals™

COLORING & ACTIVITY BOOK

KAPPA Books

Visit us at www.kappapublishing.com/kappabooks

Lost Chick

Baby Chick is lost from the farm. Can you help him find his way back?

Me and My Shadow

Draw a line from Bernard to match his shadow.

A

B

C

D

Tractor Madness

Count how many tractors there are
and write the number in the box.

What's Wrong Goat?

Circle the letter of the goat that doesn't belong.

A

B

C

D

Oink! Oink!

Connect the dots to find out who is oinking at you.

Muddy Fun

Use the color chart below to color in the picture.

A = PINK B = BLUE C = BROWN D = YELLOW

Owlin' Around

There a five things different between the two pictures.
Circle the differences.

Feelin' Sheepish

Finish drawing the sheep in the box.

Favorite Barnyard Pals

Use the words in the box to fill in the puzzle grid.

DUCKS
PIGS
HORSES
COWS
ROOSTER

Farm Facts

Cross out letters that appear more than four times and write the remaining letters on the lines to finish the fun fact.

No two cows have exactly the

X	S	B	A	Y	I	Z	M
E	I	C	H	B	P	X	U
Y	C	A	X	T	X	H	T
Z	E	U	R	I	Y	N	I
O	B	Y	Z	F	X	Y	H
X	H	C	U	B	S	C	X
Z	I	P	X	C	X	X	O
I	B	U	T	Y	H	S	Z

___ ___ ___ ___

___ ___ ___ ___ ___ ___ ___

___ ___   ___ ___ ___ ___ ___

Rabbit's Mate

Circle the letter of the shadow that matches Roger's shape.

A B C D

Fun Pig Facts

I bet you didn't know...

Happy pigs rest for over 82% of the day.

Pigs don't sweat like humans, so they roll around in the mud to cool off. The mud also protects their skin from sunburn and insect bites.

Pigs enjoy close contact with people. Most love to be scratched behind the ears and shoulders and will happily roll over for a belly rub.

Piglets love playing with balls and other toys, and they have fun playing chase with each other.

Pigs have tested higher on intelligence tests than most other animals.

Missing Vowels

Using only the vowels A, O, and E, fill in the missing letters on the blanks.

D _ N K _ Y

G _ _ T

R _ _ S T _ R

Secret Spot

Lead Harry Horse and his pal Ronnie Rooster
to their favorite spot on the farm.

Gobble Gobble!

Circle the letter of the turkey that matches Tommy Turkey.

CHICKENS
RULE

Holy Cow!

Connect the dots to finish the cow.

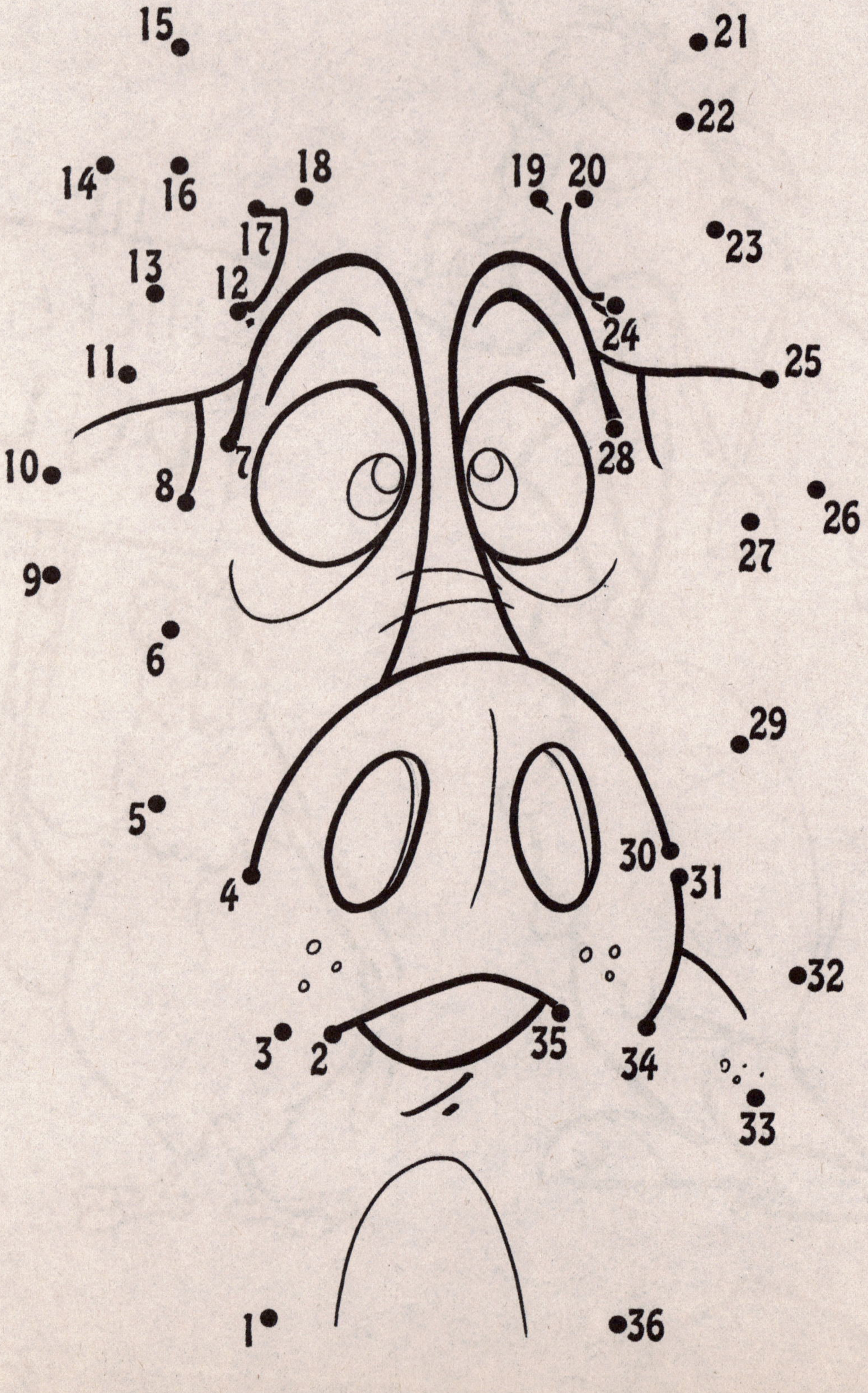

Farm Art

In the scene below draw what your barn would look like if you had one.

A Herd of Cows

Count how many cows are on the page
and write the number in the box.

A Puzzling Rooster

Draw a line from each piece of the rooster to where it belongs in the puzzle.

Farm Fun Dominos

Circle the domino tile that does NOT match another tile.

Crossout

Cross out the pictures that answers the statements below.
Circle the farm animal that is left.

Cross out if you have horns.
Cross out if you have a snout.
Cross out if you have a beak.

A Goat's Treat

Use the box below to solve the code and find out an interesting fact about goats.

Goats are extremely

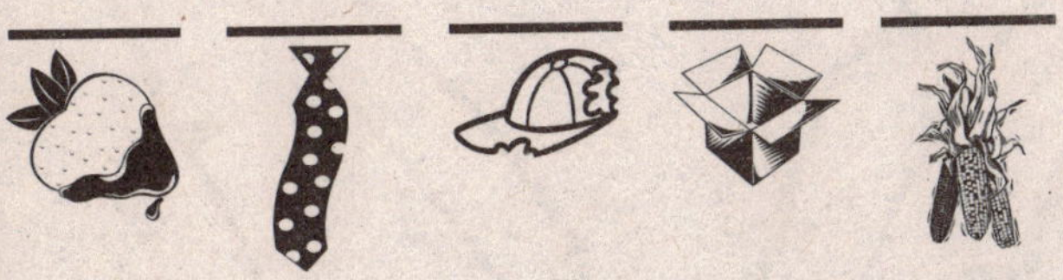 

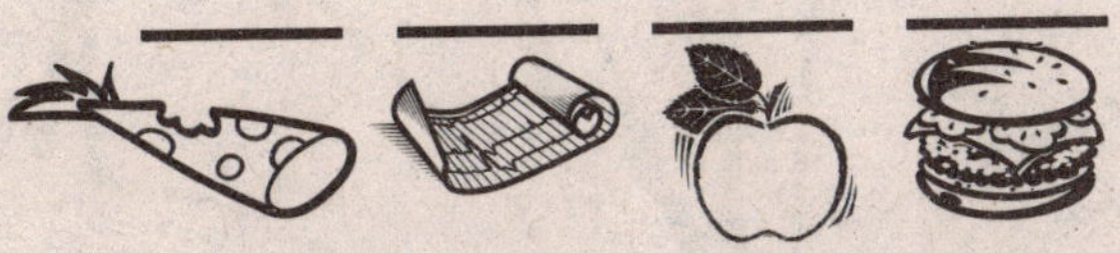 

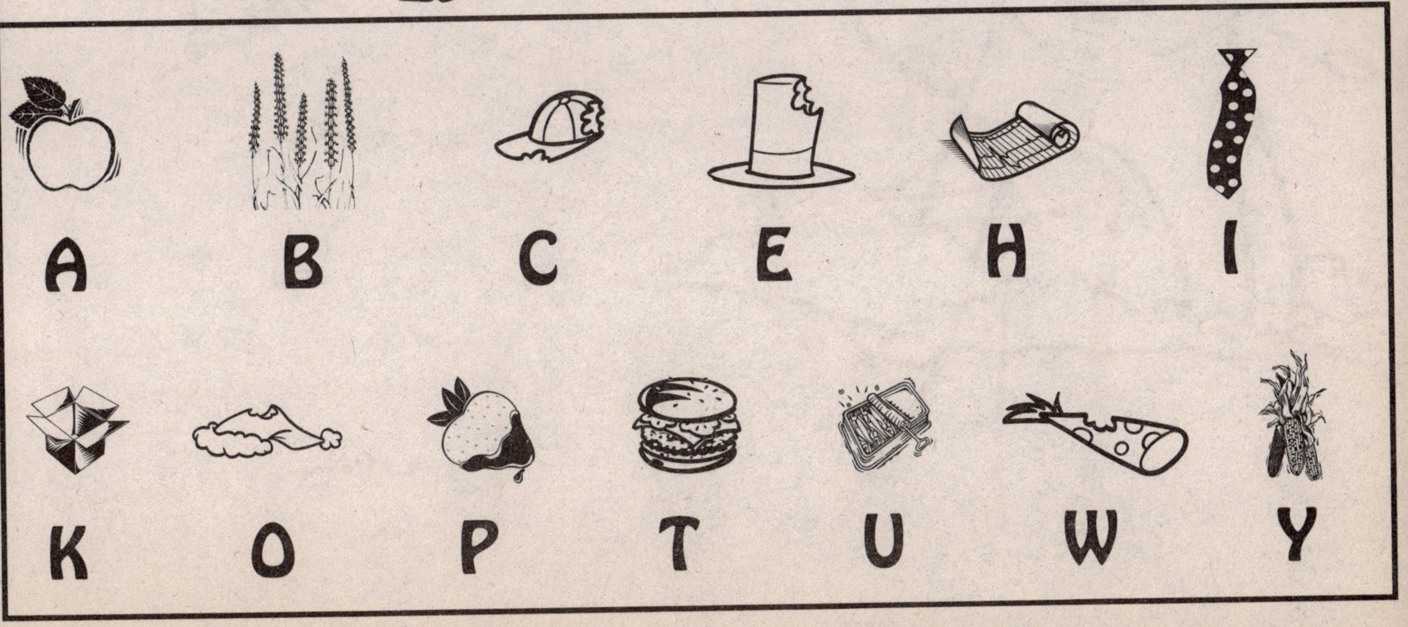

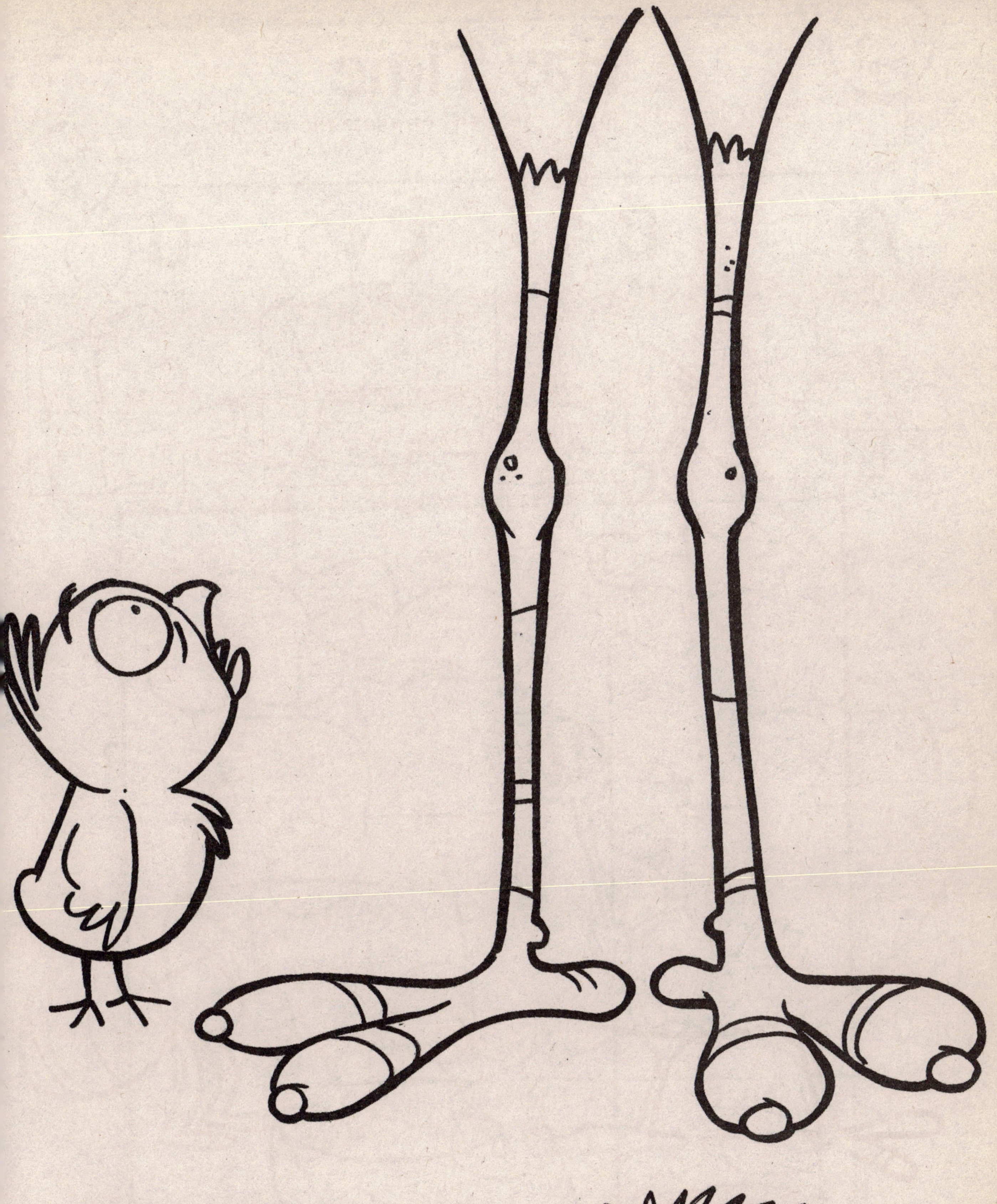

Hay Time

Circle the puzzle piece to complete the puzzle.

A

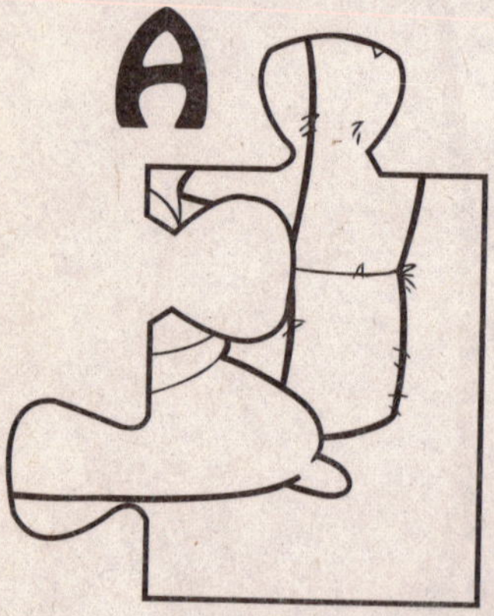

B

C

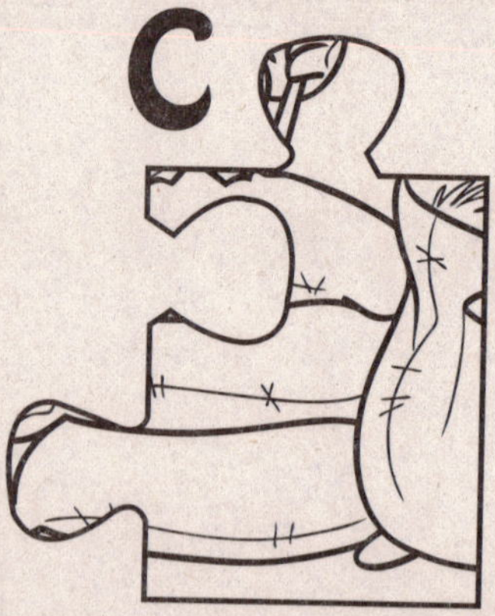

D

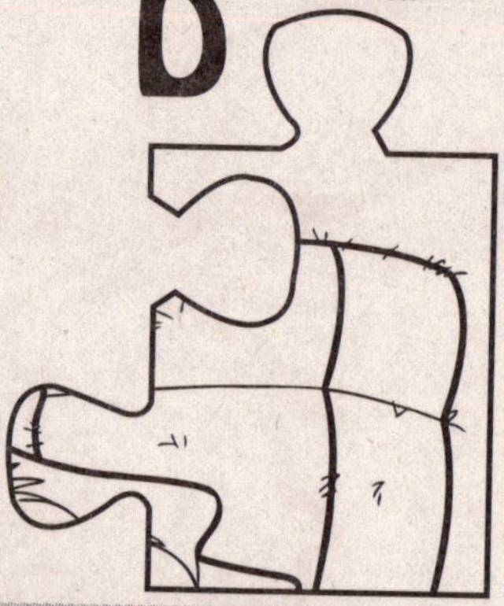

Word Play

Write on the lines all the words you can make out of the following:

CHICKEN COOP

Hen

Fun Cow Facts

I bet you didn't know...

A cow stands up and sits down about 14 times a day.

Cows do not bite grass; rather they curl their tongue around it.

A cow can climb up the stairs, but cannot climb down. This is because her knees cannot bend properly.

Cows can drink up to 35 gallons of water a day.

Cows have a single stomach, but four digestive compartments.

Cows have an acute sense of smell and can smell something up to 6 miles away.

Lost Traveler

Circle the five differences between the pictures.

Adding Up

Add the number of pictures together
and write the answer in the box.

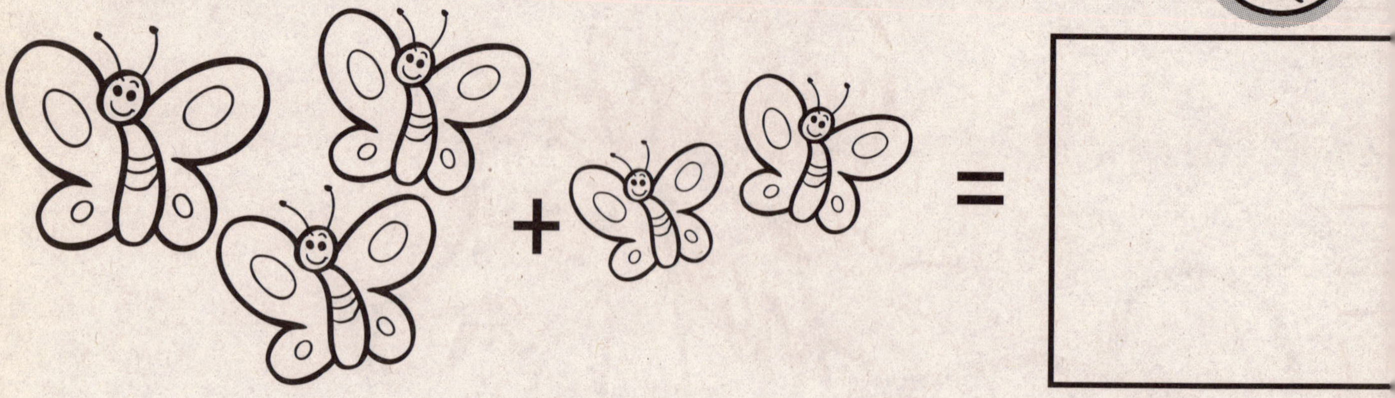

Party at the Pond

Can you help Gretta Goose find her way to the party at the pond?

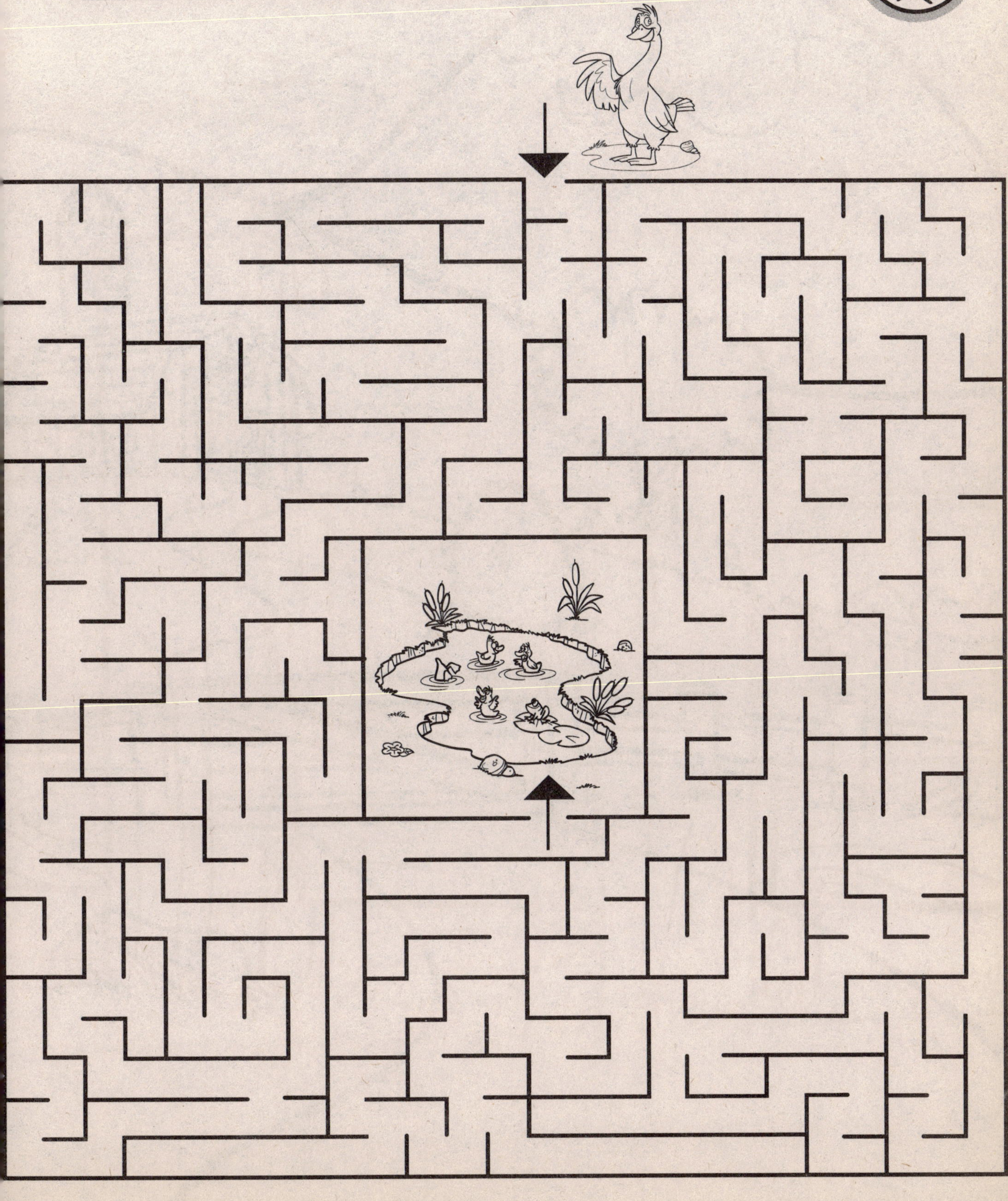

Z Z Z Z Z z

Doodle Doodle Doo

Use the grid on the picture to help
you draw your own chick.

Farm Words

Use the words in the word bank to fill in the crosspatch.

HAY
FARMER
GRAIN
CHICKEN

Missing Vowels

Using only the vowels I, E, and O, fill in the missing letters on the blanks.

H __ RS __

SH __ __ P

CH __ CK __ N

Down on the Farm

On the lines below write a story about how you would run a farm.

ANSWERS

Lost Chick

Me and My Shadow

D

Tractor Madness

8

What's Wrong Goat?

C

Oink! Oink!

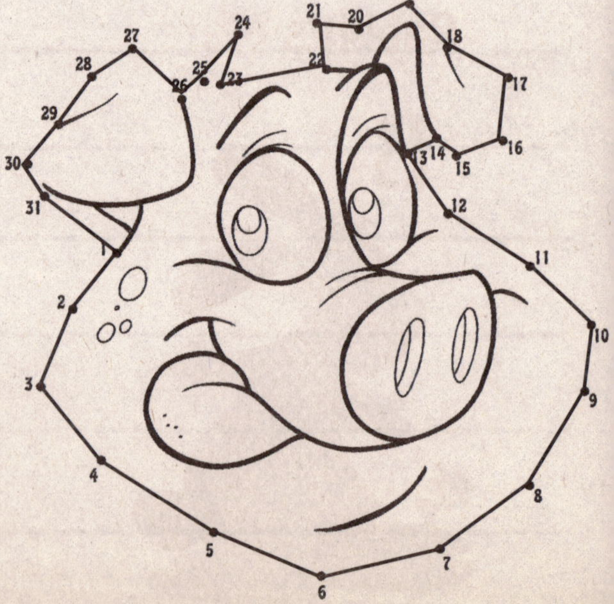

ANSWERS

Owlin' Around

Favorite Barnyard Pals

			P			
			I			H
	C		G			O
R	O	O	S	T	E	R
	W					S
	S					E
		D	U	C	K	S

Farm Facts

S A M E
P A T T E R N
O F S P O T S

Rabbit's Mate

B

Missing Vowels

DoNKeY

GoaT

RooSTeR

ANSWERS

Secret Spot

Gobble Gobble!

Holy Cow!

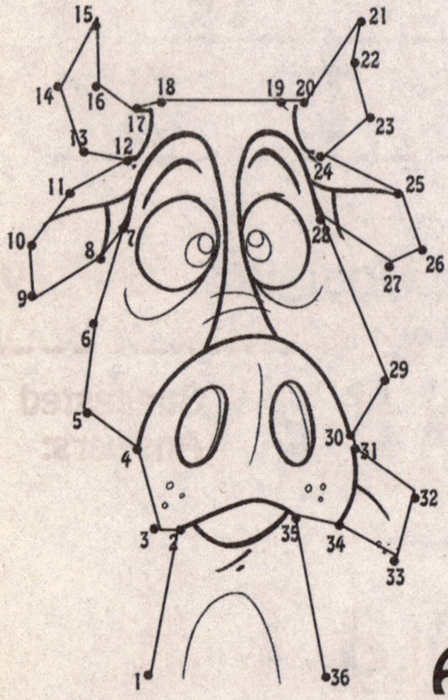

A Puzzling Rooster

A Herd of Cows

12

ANSWERS

Farm Fun Dominos

Crossout

A Goat's Treat

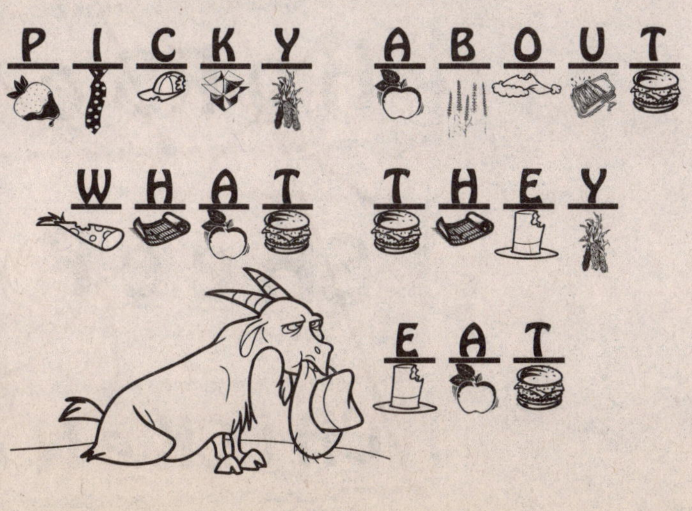

Hay Time

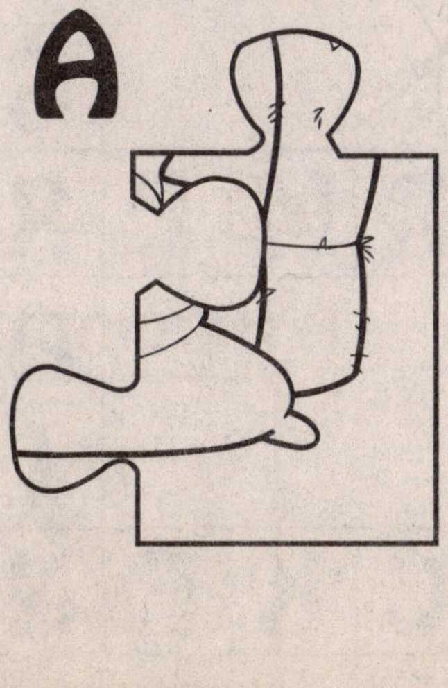

Word Play

CHICKEN COOP

Suggested Answers:

Poke
Neck
Chick
Pick
Chin
Hip
Chip
Pen
Chop

ANSWERS

Lost Traveler

Adding Up

5
3
4

Party at the Pond

Farm Words

		H				G
	F	A	R	M	E	R
		Y				A
						I
C	H	I	C	K	E	N

Missing Vowels

H o RS e

SH e e P

CH i CK e N